# Table of Contents

# Introduction

With the price of solar components on a steady decline over the past 10 years, there has never been a better time to take part in the Government of Ontario's solar Feed In Tariff program (FIT, or microFIT). Through my years of education in alternative energy, trained as an Alternative Energy Engineering Technologist, and then working for the past five years in the booming solar industry in Ontario, I have heard from many people that the reason that they don't proceed with a solar installation is because of the paperwork involved.

This book is designed to show the entire process, step by step, to make it simple to apply for and obtain an application approval for a microFIT contract offer with the Independent Electrical Safety Operators (IESO), formerly known as the Ontario Power Authority (OPA) prior to 2015.

The other agency that you will be dealing with later on in order to participate in the microFIT program is your local distribution company (LDC). Your LDC is simply the company who sends you hydro bills, for example Hydro One, (and they will also be the ones sending you cheques/direct deposits for your microFIT system). The LDC paperwork cannot be filled out until after the microFIT team approves your application, at which time they will ask you to submit a connection request to your LDC. The paperwork for this varies widely with each LDC (there are about 70 of them in Ontario), and are beyond the scope of this book. See my upcoming book entitled "How to submit hydro paperwork for a solar application in Ontario: Step-by-step instructions for submitting a microFIT or net metering application with your LDC", which will be available as an e-book or paperback on Amazon, likely by the time you are reading this and ready for that step.

While many solar companies will offer to complete the paperwork process on your behalf with no obligation (which I have done as part of my professional career for the past half-decade), I can understand that some do not want to be somewhat excluded from the process, and feel that they have to rely on that company throughout. Many might feel an obligation to continue with the company who did all that work for them in obtaining the approval, as I might feel a certain obligation to purchase a car from a dealership where I took a test-drive of a vehicle and had the salesman spend a few hours explaining all the details of the car and setting up the paperwork for me.

There is no obligations or contracts you have to sign, little to no costs, and amazingly little time involved, in order to apply and get a microFIT contract offer, so you can at that point decide whether you want to move forward and build a system, at which point you can shop your contract around to various installers (which usually will offer a discounted price if you have the paperwork done and are potentially ready to build as soon as you sign on the dotted line), or else decide at that point you don't want to move ahead, and that's entirely up to you, there's no commitment or repercussions to not moving forward.

For the past five years, the microFIT program has undergone some changes, but throughout that time up until present, and at least until 2016, the application window is open to anyone at any time. What differentiates the microFIT program from the FIT program is the size of your system. A microFIT system is limited to 10kW as its maximum size (for example, 40 solar panels x 250W each), and is designed for residential and agricultural markets, whereas the FIT program is anything above that size. Note the FIT program offers lower rates (because of the scalability factor as prices per Watt decrease with size), but the application window is only open once a year for a short period of time, and the available contracts are highly oversubscribed (only about 50% of FIT applications were approved in the last two application windows). The microFIT program, on the other hand, has never reached the yearly capacity set aside for it, so there is no competition for contracts.

So without further ado, let's get started on what you will need in order to apply.

## Parcel Register

This is the only document that many people do not have on hand, and as such is the only cost involved in applying for and obtaining a microFIT contract offer. A parcel register is an official and legal document describing your property and the legal owner(s) of it, stored at the Ontario Land Registry. If you don't already have a copy of your parcel register, you will need to go to your local Land Registry office and ask for a copy. These Land Registry offices are located in many ServiceOntario locations, please see Appendix A for a complete listing of Land Registry office locations in Ontario. This will cost you $8 to obtain, and you will need to scan a copy of it as you are required to download it at the time you make your microFIT application.

Another option if you know someone in real estate, or have recently purchased your home from a realtor, is to reach out to them and see if they have access to a web-based program called Geowarehouse. The real estate industry uses this extensively in Ontario, and from the website you are able to download an electronic copy of your parcel register directly. Note, however, that to obtain this online through the Geowarehouse site the cost is $28 plus HST.

The microFIT program is designated for individuals, farmers, and a few types of organizations (basically, it excludes businesses from participating), so the main purpose in being required to submit your parcel register is to determine whether you are an eligible participant. If, for example, you know your property is registered under "XYZ Corporation Inc.", and that is what will appear on your parcel register, then your application will be rejected. If that is the case, you could submit a request at your Land Registry office to transfer the property into your name and/or each individual in the business's names, eg. "Mrs. X., Mr. Y, Mr. Z". Once that change takes effect, you would then be eligible to apply for a microFIT, even if the building is strictly a commercial building/enterprise. The downside to this is that the property may be in that corporation's name for tax/other purposes, if so or if you're unsure, speak with a lawyer or accountant to determine the ramifications of changing your property ownership.

The following chart shows how is eligible to participate in the microFIT program, with examples.

## Who is eligible to participate in the microFIT program based on Owner as listed on Parcel Register

| Ownership type | Examples | Eligible? |
|---|---|---|
| Individual(s) | Jane Doe ; Jane Doe and John Deere | YES |
| Farmer | Acme Farms Inc. | YES* |
| Farm or Renewable Energy Co-operative | Must be incorporated under the Co-operative Corporations Act | YES |
| Municipality | City of Toronto ; Region of Waterloo | YES |
| LDC Participant | Hydro One ; Enersource | YES |
| Schools | Toronto District School Board ; McMaster University | YES** |
| Hospitals or Long-Term Care Homes | Toronto General Hospital ; Sunny Acres Long Term Care Home | YES** |
| Aboriginal Community | Any First Nation that is a "band" ; the Metis Nation of Ontario | YES |
| Social Housing or Affordable Housing | Toronto Community Housing | YES** |
| Faith-based Organization | St. Patrick's Church ; The Islamic Centre of Toronto | YES** |
| Corporation | Big Box Store Inc. | NO |

*a Farmer/Farm entity is eligible as long as it has a valid Farm Business Registration Number

**additional restrictions/requirements can apply, please see Appendix B for more details

Please note, if your parcel register lists a number of individual people, each of those people will need to be applicants (it only involves a few extra lines to be filled in with your application). Be aware, if even one individual on that parcel register already has a microFIT contract in their name from another property, then you are no longer eligible to participate in the microFIT program. Current as of 2015, the option is to have that person removed from the parcel register at the Land Registry Office, or, alternatively, one of the proposed upcoming changes to the microFIT program is to allow individuals to own more than one microFIT property (provided the solar photovoltaic system is on a separate property of course), so beginning in 2016 it may be possible to apply.

So with this knowledge and an electronic copy of your parcel register, you're now ready to begin your microFIT application. The first step you will need to take is to register for a microFIT account.

## Registering for a microFIT Account

Registering for a microFIT account is simple; simply go to https://mymicrofit.powerauthority.on.ca/sign-up.php , or search for "microFIT registration" and follow the link, and begin filling out the information. Any fields marked with a "*" are mandatory. Here's the list of information required and how to fill it out:

**Username:** Here you can choose any username you like, as long as it is not already taken by someone else.

**Password:** Choose anything that you will remember, it must be between 8 and 20 characters long. Your password will also need to contain an uppercase letter, a lowercase letter, a letter, and a symbol (one of the symbols above the numbers on your keyboard). You will also need to **Confirm Password** again in the next field, so type the same password in again. You will know that your password strength is good enough when the red text below the password field disappears. I'd highly recommend writing down your username and password somewhere, but if you do forget there's a way to obtain it again through your e-mail.

**Legal Name of Registrant:** This is the first place where your parcel register comes in- make sure to copy exactly the full text off the parcel register, spelling mistakes, maiden names, and all.

**Primary Contact First Name / Last Name:** These fields will be the person you want to be the primary (and often only) person the IESO will contact with any questions or updates, and will assumedly be yourself since you are reading this. This primary contact does not need to necessarily be an individual listed on the parcel register, for example, when I complete these for other people I put in my own name and contact information here.

**Primary Contact Email:** For this one it's important to use an e-mail address you can and do access on a regular basis, as this will usually be the only way the IESO will contact you. Also, if you forget your username or password, it is to this e-mail address that the reset link will be sent to. Later on you are able to change this e-mail address.

**Address, City/Town, Country, Provice/State/Region, Postal/ZIP Code**: Fill in this information with your mailing address, which is not necessarily the project address. Again if you move you can change this information in the future, and anyway it is very rare for the IESO to send you anything in the mail, all communication takes place via e-mail and your microFIT home page.

**Phone Number/Extension:** I have never been contacted via telephone, but it is mandatory to include your phone number here.

**Challenge Question/Answer**: The web page provides a drop-down menu with a few choices to set up as a question that will be asked to you if you forget your password or want to change your account information that you filled in above at some point in the future. My only recommendation here is to choose a question that has a static answer, eg. if you have 10 aunts, don't select the "What is the first name of your favourite aunt?", or, even worse, "What is the name of your favourite movie?". Ten years from now if you want to make changes, you might not remember, so I'd suggest "What is your mother's maiden name?" or "What was your first pet's name?" so the Challenge Answer you put in won't change over time.

The last step to register for a microFIT account is to fill in the jumbled up letters and or numbers at the bottom of the screen in the field below it-this is just to prove you're not a computer program randomly creating microFIT accounts.  Once that's done, click the 'Submit' button at the bottom of the page.

If there are any errors or missing information, you will stay on the same page, so scroll through the information you entered and see what's missing, otherwise, you will proceed to the Terms of Use Page.  At the bottom of this page, you must check off the 'I agree to the above terms and conditions' and then hit the 'Submit Registration' button.

Congratulations, you now have a microFIT account, but in order to activate it you must go to your e-mail account that you entered above and open the message sent from "The microFIT Team".  It should arrive within a couple minutes, else check your Junk Email folder.  Click on the link in the e-mail, or copy and paste it into your web browser's address bar, and you will be directed to the microFIT site with a message that thanks you for registering.  There will also be a FIT registration ID, starting with FIT- ..., I would suggest writing this number down as well, although it appears on your microFIT home page as well.

You are now able to log in to your account, and create a microFIT application for your property.

## Logging in to your microFIT home page and starting your application

To log in to your microFIT home page, go to: https://mymicrofit.powerauthority.on.ca/login.php, or search for "microFIT login", and enter the Username and Password that you set up when registering your account, and enter the wavy characters (captcha) shown in the box in the field below it, and then click on the 'Login' button.

Note this is also the screen where if you forget your username or password for your account, you can click on the applicable links to find or reset them.

You will now be directed to your microFIT home page, which links to the rest of the site. The three option bars at the top are 'HOME' – the screen you are currently on, 'MY PROFILE', which allows you to change your username, password, primary contact information, or your challenge question and answer, as well as a 'LOGOUT' button that will close your homepage and require you to log back in to add or access any information, which is important if you're doing this on a public or shared computer.

Along the right hand side of your home page, you will see your Registration ID, and below that, a box titled 'My microFIT Messages' which will also display the number of unread messages you have. When the IESO communicates with you (via your primary e-mail address you registered with), they will not include information, they will only send you an e-mail telling you that you have a new microFIT message. In order to find out what that message is, you will need to click on the 'My microFIT

Messages' link to see the message. At this point, you will have 0 messages as you haven't created an application yet, which brings us to the next button below, which is 'Create an Application'.

When you're ready to begin, click the 'Create an Application' button. Note these pages time out after several minutes, so if you need to step away for a few minutes or gather some more information, you are able to save the data for each step when you click the 'SAVE AND CONTINUE' button.

The microFIT application has 8 steps, some are just a simple click, some require a bit more time and information- next are the 8 steps and how to complete them in order.

## microFIT application – Step 1

On this page, there is a list of the eligible participant types, so click on the button next to the one that applies to you (based on the owner's name/type on your parcel register), eg. Individual, Farmer, etc., and then click the 'SAVE AND CONTINUE' button.

## microFIT application – Step 2

The information requested on this page will vary depending on the type of applicant you selected in Step 1, so see the relevant sub-section below that applies to you.

### Step 2 – Individual

The first thing you will need to enter is the name and date of birth of all of the individuals listed on the parcel register. Be sure to enter the first and middle name(s), as well as the last name, exactly as it appears on the parcel register.

Below the name box is the Date of Birth, if you click on the empty field a calendar will pop up, letting you scroll to the year, month, and date.

Below that is a link that allows you to 'Add another Applicant'. If you have more than one person listed on the parcel register, you must 'Add another Applicant' for each additional person that's listed.

Once you've completed that, you will need to fill in the contact information again similar to what you did when you registered for your microFIT account. Note this information must be the contact information of one of the applicants listed on the parcel register, so if you're completing this as someone other than one of the applicants themselves, you will need to enter their information here and not your own, as per below:

**Primary Applicant:** Fill in the first, middle, and last name of the individual exactly as it appears on the parcel register. Note if there's more than one individual, select one of the people to be the primary applicant (presumably yourself). There's no additional benefits or privileges to being listed as the primary applicant, other than you will be the main point of contact with the IESO. If there is more than one individual, you will need to fill out an additional piece of paperwork at a later step, but we'll go into details on that when we get to that step in the process.

**Primary Email Address:** this again will be the e-mail address that the IESO correspondence will go to, so I recommend using the same e-mail address you used to register for your account.

**Secondary Email Address:** this is optional, but if you have a second person on your account you can add their e-mail address here.

**Phone Number:** enter the same phone number you included when you registered, and don't expect to ever receive a call.

**Mailing Address:** enter the mailing address of the primary applicant (likely the same one you entered when you registered). This does not have to be the property address you're applying for a microFIT for, just where you want to receive any mail, but again, don't expect to ever get physical mail for your project.

Click 'SAVE AND CONTINUE' to go to Step 3.

*Step 2 – Farmer*

This will be the same as for an individual, so see that section above, with the addition that you will also need to enter your Farm Business Registration Number. Instead of an applicant name and birthday, you select 'Other Farming Entity' in question 1.1.1, and type in the name of your farm as per your parcel register.

### Step 2 – Farm or Renewable Energy Co-operative

This will be the same as for an individual, so see that section above, except that the **Name of Applicant:** will be the legal name of the Co-operative, and the owner as listed on the parcel register for the property will be the **Host Member**.

### Step 2 – Municipality

This will be the same as for an individual, except the Name of Applicant will be the legal name of the municipality as it appears on the parcel register.

### Step 2 – LDC Participant

If you're an LDC, you've done this many times and won't be reading this book.

### Step 2 – University

This will be the same as applying as an individual as per above, except that instead of typing in an Applicant Name, you will need to select one of the eligible universities from the drop-down menu.

*Step 2 – School or College*

This will be the same as applying as an individual as per above, except that the name of the Applicant will be the name of the School or College, and you will need to select whether the applicant is: an elementary school or secondary school, a school board or school authority, or a college.

*Step 2 – Hospital or Long-Term Care Home*

This will be the same as applying as an individual as per above, except that the name of the Applicant will be the name of the Hospital or Long-Term Care Home, and you will need to select whether the applicant is: a public hospital, a private hospital, or a long-term care home.

*Step 2 – Aboriginal Community*

This will be the same as applying as an individual as per above, except that you will also need to select that either: 1) a First Nation "band", and then choose the Band Name from the drop-down menu.
2) the Métis Nation of Ontario, and choose the applicable Métis Community from the drop-down menu.
3) a Person, other than a natural person, that is determined by the Government of Ontario to represent the collective interests of a community that is composed of Métis or other aboriginal individuals, and then provide a description in the field below, or

4) a corporation that is wholly-owned by one or more Aboriginal Communities, and then enter the Legal Name of Applicant in the field below.

### Step 2 – Social Housing or Affordable Housing

This will be the same as applying as an individual as per above, except that you will also need to select that the Applicant is either: an owner or less of social housing, or an owner or lessee of affordable housing. The Name of Applicant will be the name on the parcel register.

### Step 2 – Faith-based Organization

This will be the same as applying as an individual as per above, except instead of a person's name, the Applicant will be the name of your organization, as listed on your parcel register.

## microFIT application – Step 3

This section is asking if you are submitting the application for yourself (as one of the property owners listed on the parcel register). If you're submitting this for someone else, you would need to select 'Yes' and fill in your contact information. If that's the case, you will also need to fill out an Applicant Declaration Form, and have each legal applicant listed on the parcel register sign this, allowing you to submit the application on their behalf. This form is downloadable at:

http://microfit.powerauthority.on.ca/sites/default/files/page/Applicant-Declaration-Natural-Person-Version3-2.pdf

If you're submitting an application on your own behalf, you don't need this form. Just leave the 'No' button selected in Question 2.1, and the rest of the data will be auto-filled with your contact information that you previously provided, so all you have to do in this section is click 'Save and Continue'.

## microFIT application – Step 4

The first question in this section asks what type of Renewable Fuel you're proposing. The one you'll have to decide between is 'Solar photovoltaic (Rooftop)', or 'Solar photovoltaic (Non-Rooftop)'.

Early on in the program, non-rooftop systems were more common; however, in recent years there has been a large push to utilize rooftops so as to not take up space that could be otherwise available for growing crops, etc. In order to facilitate the shift towards rooftop solar, the rates were adjusted so that rooftop solar contracts were offered more money than non-rooftop solar types. Another restriction that has taken effect is that if your property is zoned residential (without agricultural), or even if an adjoining property to yours is zoned residential, you are not eligible for a ground-mount microFIT. If you are planning on a ground-mount solar system, there are additional steps that need to be taken.

For ground-mount (Non-Rooftop) solar applications, you will also need to have a 'Zoning Opinion' filled out by a Professional Planner or equivalent, or else a 'Zoning Form' filled out by chief building official, municipal chief administrative officer, municipal clerk or equivalent municipal official for your area. Once completed, you will need to submit this document online with your microFIT application. These documents are available for download on the microFIT website. If you're planning on a rooftop installation, you can disregard this.

For Question **3.2 Name of proposed microFIT Project**: You can enter anything you want. If you're not feeling creative just call it *YourLastName* Solar.

Question **3.3: Nameplate Capacity of the proposed microFIT Project (in kW):** Is asking what size of a system you want, from 0 to 10kW. If you're not sure what size, you can go for the full 10kW (so enter '10' in the field. It's much easier to decrease your system size than to increase it later. If you want a rough idea of the size, look at the room available on your south, east, and west roof facings. For grid-tied solar panels, there are two basic sizes, 60-cell and 72-cell panels. Solar panels are made from solar cells soldered together, and are 6 wide on the short side, so a 60-cell panel has ten rows of 6, while a 72-cell panel just has an extra two rows of 6 (12 in total), so it will be longer. A typical 60-cell solar panel will 5'6" x 3'3", and a 72-cell panel will be 6'6" x 3'3". Figure out roughly how many solar panels will fit on your available roof space, and then multiply by 0.25kW [i.e. 250W] per 60 cell panel, or by 0.3kW per 72 cell panel. Yes, there are higher wattage panels available, but they can come at a premium, and these numbers are standard for estimating purposes.

> *Sample calculation estimating the size of your system:*
> Roof height 20', roof length 30'
> 3 rows of 72-cell panels = 6'6" x 3 = 19' 6" (fits)
> 30' roof length / 3'3" per panel = 9.23 = 9 panels
> 3 rows of 9 panels = 27 panels
> 27 panels x 0.3kW = 8.1kW
> Round to nearest kW = 8 kW

Question **3.4: Will the proposed microFIT project Project be connected to a battery back-up or supply system?** The answer is No. You're generally not allowed to connect your microFIT system to a battery bank or supply system, because then you could buy extra power at a lower rate, then feed it out through your microFIT system at your much higher contract rate. If you're looking for an off-grid solution, then you don't need to apply for a microFIT. Click 'Save and Continue'.

## microFIT application – Step 5

The first question, **4.1: The property is located on:** You will select 'Property owned by Applicant', unless the property is located on a Reserve or Special Reserve lands, in which case you would select that box.

**Question 4.2 to 4.4** are where you need to have a copy of your parcel register handy.

For Project Address, this has to of course be the address where you want to have a microFIT on, which may or may not be your mailing address as well. Enter your Street Number, Unit/Suite/Apt number if applicable, as well as your Street Name.

From the drop-down menu under Street Type, select the applicable option, eg. Avenue, Line, Street, etc. Do not include this in your street name. By that I mean do not put 'Main Street' under Street Name, then select 'Street' under Street Type. Instead, put 'Main' under Street Name, and select 'Street' from the Street Type drop-down menu. If you have a Street Type not listed under the other options, select 'Other'.

If you have a direction on your street name, eg. Main Street West, choose from the options available under 'Street Direction', otherwise leave it at the default 'Select One' option.

The next part, Legal Description, leaves you a large box to fill in the legal description of your property, and is the most common mistake to make when filling out a microFIT application. From your parcel register, you must enter the description exactly as it appears. See Appendix C: Sampe Parcel register, to be sure what information you're to fill out here. The legal description will be near the top of the page, and likely contain words like: PT LT 1, CON 2, CITY, etc., etc. and is usually fairly long. Fill in the text as it appears, with punctuation and line spaces exactly as they appear on your parcel.

Below that, you will enter your City of Township, as well as Postal Code.

For **4.3. Project Municipality:** Select yours from the drop-down box provided.

For **4.4. Property Identification Number (PIN):** enter your PIN number from your parcel register.
Your PIN number is located near the top of your parcel, and will contain five numbers followed by a dash '-', and then have four more numbers. If there's any letters trailing after those nine numbers, ignore them, all you are to enter are the five numbers, then a dash, then the last four numbers, with no spacing in between, eg. '12345-6789'.

Once this is done, double check you've copied the legal description and PIN number correctly, then hit 'Save and Continue'. The hardest part is done.

## microFIT application – Step 6

This section is where you fill out your hydro information for your property. You'll need a copy of your bill or similar to fill this out.

For **5.1. Local Distribution Company:** Select the appropriate option from the drop-down list.

For **5.2 and 5.3:** Pull out a hydro bill and enter the name and account number exactly as it appears on your bill. Don't worry if the name on your hydro bill doesn't match one or any of the names you're applying for, that doesn't matter. The name and account number will typically be at or near the top of page 1 of your invoice.

## microFIT application – Step 7

This step is where you need to upload any applicable documents. The web page will ask for the files that you will need to upload, which varies depending on the type of application you submitted. To upload I file, click the 'Browse' button, which will open a window on your computer where you can search for your file. I suggest keeping the documents in their own folder on your desktop so they're easy to find. Once you have the file listed on the web page, hit 'Upload' to submit it. You'll know you've successfully uploaded the file when it has a date and time stamp beside it. If you accidentally choose the wrong file, click the red 'X' button that appears to the right of your file.

Note the files will need to be in .pdf format. If your scanner uploads them as a picture file, eg. jpg, gif, etc., open the file and select 'Save as', and choose 'pdf' from the options. If your program doesn't offer this option, there are many free online website converters such as http://www.pdfonline.com/convert-jpg-to-pdf that will let you upload your document and convert it to pdf. A quick search on google will give you access to hundreds of these free tools.

Also note that the maximum file size for each document to upload on the microFIT application is 5 MB, so if necessary turn down the resolution of your scanner. Another option could be to just take a picture on your phone of the hard copy document and e-mail it to yourself-you'll want to make sure the entire document shows up though and that it of good quality.

The documents that you are required to upload vary depending on the type of applicant you previously selected:

*If you submitted as either a single individual, farmer/farming entity, municipality, university, school or college, or as a faith-based organization,* you will just need to upload your Parcel Register, then hit 'Save and Continue'.

*If you submitted as more than one individuals or farmers/farming entities*, you will need to upload your Parcel Register as well as an 'Additional Contact Information Form'. These forms are available at:

http://microfit.powerauthority.on.ca/sites/default/files/page/Additional-Contact-Information-Version3-2.pdf

On this form, just complete the contact info for any additional persons/farmers that are listed as applicants, ie. 2nd, 3rd, 4th, etc. applicant information. You do not fill in the primary contact information (yours), as that information was already filled out during the application process. Once done, scan the file and upload it, the other applicants signatures are not required. Once both files are uploaded, hit 'Save and Continue'.

*If you submitted as a Farm or Renewable Energy Co-operative,* you will need to upload your parcel register, the Articles of Incorporation for your co-operative, the Certificate of Incorporation of your co-operative, as well as the Consent of Host Member document. You will need to get these documents from your co-operative to upload them and submit your microFIT application.

*If you submitted as an LDC Participant,* then you've done this many times and will not be reading this book.

*If you submitted as a Hospital or Long-Term Care Home,* you will need to upload your parcel register. If you selected 'Private Hospital' in Step 2, you will also need to upload a copy of your Ontario license issued under the Private Hospitals Act. If you selected 'a long-term care home', in Step 2, you will need to upload a copy of your license, issued under the Long-Term Care Homes Act, 2007.

*If you submitted as an Aboriginal Community,* then you will just need to upload your parcel register, unless you have selected 'a corporation that is wholly-owned by one or more Aboriginal Communities' in Step 2-if so, then you will also need to upload your Articles of Incorporation and your Shareholders' Register.

*If you submitted as Social Housing or Community Housing,* then you will need to submit your parcel register. In addition to the following, depending on what you selected in Step 2:
If you selected 'an owner or less of social housing' in Step 2, you will also have to upload a Funding Agreement (unless you're listed under the Housing Services Act in Schedules 1-47 of O.Reg 368/11).

If you selected 'an owner or lessee of affordable housing' in Step 2, you will need to upload a copy of the Funding Agreement or a copy of the Mortgage Charge.

## microFIT application – Step 8

You've done it-you're at the final step in the application process! This step is just a review that shows all the information you've submitted in the previous steps in the application. After making sure everything is correct, you can print or save a copy of your application by clicking the 'Print Summary' button. If there are any errors, select the '<<Previous' button, and go back through the pages and make any necessary changes. Note even if you have to back to Step 1, don't despair- the information you filled out and uploaded will still be saved, so make the change then keep clicking 'Save and Continue' until you're back at this last step.

Once you're satisfied you have everything right, click 'Save and Continue'. This will take you to a page where you have to agree to a bunch of standard conditions that vary depending on the type of application you submitted. Read them, and then you need to check off each box, and then hit 'Submit Application to the IESO'.

You will then get a message saying thanks for submitting your application, etc. etc. You can then go back to your home page, where you will see your microFIT application has now been given a FIT reference number. This FIT reference number is **different** from your FIT registration number. Think of your FIT registration number (the one you get when you register for an account), as a number that represents your overall account. The FIT reference number, on the other hand, is tagged to a specific application.

To help clear up the difference, pretend you applied to the microFIT program months or years ago, but then decided you weren't ready to move forward with a project at that time. If you log in to the microFIT site with the same username and password when you're now submitting a new application, your Registration Number will stay the same, but each application on your my microFIT homepage will have a different Reference Number.

Knowing which is which is important, as when you submit an application to your LDC, they will ask for either just your microFIT reference number, or else both your microFIT reference number as well as your microFIT registration number.

Going back to your homepage, you will see that you now have 1 unread message in the My microFIT messages section. You can read it (I recommend doing that so it goes back to 0 unread so you know if there's been any further progress on your application when you login in the future); it will just say that your application has been submitted. You'll also have an e-mail sent to your primary e-mail address saying that you have a new microFIT message.

## Conclusion

At this point, there's nothing to do but wait. The microFIT team will review your application, and get back to you (usually within a couple weeks to a month) letting you know that your application has been deemed complete, or else that there were errors on your application-usually stating what those errors were so you can fix them, and that your application has been unlocked for editing. Of course, the message will only appear in your microFIT home page, but you will notified that there has been progress by way of a message from the microFIT team to your primary e-mail address, so you can then login and see what the message says.

If you're feeling stuck or unsure, or don't understand any error messages you're getting, please feel free to drop me a line on my blog http://solarguru.weebly.com and I'll get back to you shortly.

Also, check out my upcoming e-book and paperback, "How to submit hydro paperwork for a solar application in Ontario: Step-by-step instructions for submitting a microFIT or net metering application with your LDC", which will be available on Amazon, likely by the time you are reading this, have your microFIT approval, and are ready for the next step.

I wish you every success in your solar endeavors, there's never been a better time to apply for a microFIT in Ontario, and the reasons for doing so have never been more important.

## Appendix A – Land Registry Office locations

| Location | Address | Phone No. |
|---|---|---|
| Algoma | 420 Queen St. E., Sault Ste. Marie | 705-253-8887 |
| Brant | 80 Wellington St., Brantford | 519-752-8321 |
| Bruce | 203 Cayley St., Walkerton | 519-881-2259 |
| Cochrane | 143 4$^{th}$ Ave., Cochrane | 705-272-5791 |
| Dufferin | 7-41 Broadway Ave., Orangeville | 519-941-1481 |
| Dundas | 8 5$^{th}$ St. W., Morrisburg | 613-543-2583 |
| Durham | 590 Rossland Rd. E., Whitby | 905-665-4007 |
| Elgin | 36-1010 Talbot St., St. Thomas | 519-631-3015 |
| Essex | 100-949 McDougal St., Windsor | 519-971-9980 |
| Frontenac | 1201 Division St., Kingston | 613-548-6767 |
| Glengarry | 101 Main St. N., Alexandria | 613-525-1315 |
| Grenville | 499 Centre St., Prescott | 613-925-3177 |
| Grey | Suites 1&2, 1555 16$^{th}$ St. E., Owen Sound | 519-376-1637 |
| Haldimand | 10 Echo St. W., Cayuga | 905-772-3531 |
| Haliburton | 12 Newcastle St., Minden | 705-286-1391 |
| Halton | 2$^{nd}$ Floor, 2800 Highpoint Dr., Milton | 905-864-3500 |
| Hastings | 109-199 Front St., Belleville | 613-968-4597 |
| Huron | 38 North St., Goderich | 519-524-9562 |
| Kenora | 220 Main St. S., Kenora | 807-468-2794 |
| Kent | 40 William St. N., Chatham | 519-352-5520 |
| Lambton | 102-700 Christina St. N., Sarnia | 519-337-2393 |
| Lanark | 2 Industrial Dr., Almonte | 613-256-1577 |
| Leeds | 7 King St. W., Brockville | 613-345-5751 |
| Lennox | 2-7 Snow Rd., Napanee | 613-354-3751 |
| Niagara | 59 Church St., St. Catharines | 905-684-6351 |
| Manitoulin | 27 Phipps St., Gore Bay | 705-282-2442 |
| Middlesex | 100 Dundas St., London | 519-675-7600 |
| Muskoka | 15 Dominion St., Bracebridge | 705-645-4415 |
| Nipissing | 111-447 McKeown Ave., North Bay | 705-497-6822 |
| Norfolk | 201-50 Frederick Hobson VC Dr., Simcoe | 519-426-2216 |
| Northumberland | 105-1005 Elgin St. W., Cobourg | 905-372-3813 |
| Ottawa-Carleton | 161 Elgin St., 4$^{th}$ Floor, Ottawa | 613-239-1230 |
| Oxford | 480 Peel St., Woodstock | 519-537-6287 |
| Parry Sound | 28 Miller St., Parry Sound | 705-746-5816 |
| Peel | 1 Gateway Blvd., Brampton | 905-874-4008 |
| Perth | 5 Huron St., Stratford | 519-271-3343 |
| Peterborough | 300 Water St., N Tower, Peterborough | 705-755-1342 |
| Prescott | 179 Main St. E., Hawkesbury | 613-636-0314 |
| Prince Edward | 1 Pitt St., Picton | 613-476-3219 |
| Rainy River | 353 Church St., Fort Frances | 807-274-5451 |

| | | |
|---|---|---|
| **Renfrew** | 400 Pembroke St. E., Pembroke | 613-732-8331 |
| **Russell** | 3-717 Notre Dame St., Embrun | 613-443-7852 |
| **Simcoe** | 114 Worsley St., Barrie | 705-725-7232 |
| **Stormont** | 2-720 14th St. W., Cornwall | 613-932-4522 |
| **Sudbury** | 300-199 Larch St., Sudbury | 705-564-4300 |
| **Timiskaming** | 375 Main St., Haileybury | 705-672-3332 |
| **Thunder Bay** | 201-189 Red River Rd., Thunder Bay | 807-343-7436 |
| **Toronto** | 420-20 Dundas St. W., Toronto | 416-314-4430 |
| **Victoria** | 322 Kent St. W., Lindsay | 705-324-4912 |
| **Waterloo** | 30 Duke St. W., 2nd Floor, Kitchener | 519-571-6043 |
| **Wellington** | 1 Stone Rd. W., Guelph | 519-826-3372 |
| **Wentworth** | 119 King St. W., 4th Floor, Hamilton | 905-521-7561 |
| **York Region** | 50 Bloomington Rd. W., Aurora | 905-713-7798 |

# Appendix B – Additional Regulations for Certain Applicant Types

-based on the microFIT Eligible Participant Schedule, additional restrictions may apply, published by the IESO at: http://microfit.powerauthority.on.ca/sites/default/files/page/El igibleParticipantSchedule-Version3-2.pdf

## University

To be eligible to participate in the microFIT program as a University, you must be one of the following:

Algoma, Brock, Carleton, College of the Dominican or Friar Preachers of Ottawa, University of Guelph, Lakehead, Laurentian, McMaster, Nipissing, Ontario College of Art & Design, University of Ontario Institute of Technology, University of Ottawa, Queen's, Royal Military College of Canada, Ryerson, University of Toronto, Trent, University of Toronto, Waterloo, or Western Ontario, Wilfred Laurier, University of Windsor, or York University

## School or College

A college governed by the Ontario College of Applied Arts and Technology Act, S.O. 2002, c. 8, Schedule F, or

An elementary or secondary school, school authority, or school board, that is governed in accordance with the Education Act, R.S.O. 1990, c. E.2

### Hospital or Long-Term Care Home

If a public hospital, it must be in accordance with the Public Hospitals Act, R.S.O. 1990, c. P.40

If a private hospital, it must be in accordance with the Private Hospitals Act, R.S.O.1990, c. P.24

If a long-term care home, it must be in accordance with the Long-Term Care Homes Act, 2007, S.O. 2007, c. 8

### Social Housing or Affordable Housing

Social housing must be either a housing project under the Housing Services Act, 2011, S.O. 2011, c. 6, Sched. 1, Schedule 1 to 47 of O. Reg. 368/11; or

a non-profit housing co-operative established under the Co-operative Corporations Act, R.S.O. 1990, c.35; or

non-profit housing operated by a church, religious organization, philanthropic organization, or a house of refuge or charitable institution as set out in subsection 3(1) of the Assessment Act, R.S.O. 1990, c. A.31, or

a non-profit corporation established under the Corporation Act, R.S.O. 1990, c. C38; or, finally, a housing project that is operated or managed by a local housing corporation that is constituted pursuant to Part IV of the Housing Services Act, 2011.

Affordable Housing is for projects funded by the Affordable Housing Program, pursuant to the Affordable Housing Program Agreement between the Province of Ontario and the Canada Mortgage and Housing Corporation, dated April 29, 2005.

**Faith-based Organization**

In order to be eligible for a microFIT, a faith-based organization must be a registered charity for the purposes of the Canadian Income Tax Act, and is registered as a religion under "charity type", by the Canada Revenue Agency.

# Appendix C – Sample Parcel Register

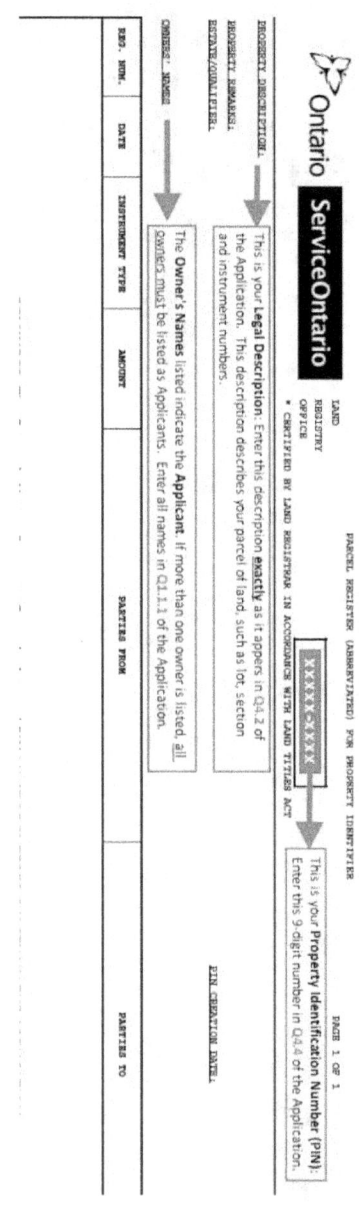